THE FIRST STONE

ALSO BY DONNA-MICHELLE ST. BERNARD

Gas Girls
A Man A Fish
Cake
Sound of the Beast
Reaching for Starlight
Indian Act: Residential School Plays (editor)
Refractions: Solo (edited with Yvette Nolan)
Refractions: Scenes (edited with Yvette Nolan)

THE FIRST STONE

BY DONNA-MICHELLE ST. BERNARD

with Music and Lyrics by Maddie Bautista

PLAYWRIGHTS CANADA PRESS

Toronto

First edition: March 2025
Printed and bound in Canada by Imprimerie Gauvin Ltée, Gatineau

Jacket art and design by Jega Delisca
Author photo by Graham Isador

Playwrights Canada Press
202-269 Richmond St. W., Toronto, ON M5V 1X1
416.703.0013 | info@playwrightscanada.com | www.playwrightscanada.com

LIBRARY AND ARCHIVES CANADA CATALOGUING IN PUBLICATION
Title: The first stone / Donna-Michelle St. Bernard.
Names: St. Bernard, Donna-Michelle, author
Description: First edition.
Identifiers: Canadiana (print) 20240532252 | Canadiana (ebook) 20240533224
| ISBN 9780369105455 (softcover) | ISBN 9780369105462 (PDF)
| ISBN 9780369105479 (EPUB)
Subjects: LCGFT: Drama.
Classification: LCC PS8637.A4525 F57 2025 | DDC C812/.6—dc23

Playwrights Canada Press staff work across Turtle Island, on Treaty 13 and Treaty 20 territories, as well as unceded lands, which are the current, ancestral, and future homes of the Anishinaabe Nations (Ojibwe / Chippewa, Odawa, Potawatomi, Algonquin, Saulteaux, Nipissing, and Mississauga / Michi Saagiig), the Wendat, members of the Haudenosaunee Confederacy (Mohawk, Oneida, Onondaga, Cayuga, Seneca, and Tuscarora), and the xʷməθkʷəy̓əm (Musqueam), Sḵwx̱wú7mesh (Squamish), and səlilwətaɬ (Tsleil-Waututh) Nations, as well as Metis and Inuit peoples. It always was and always will be Indigenous land.

We acknowledge the financial support of the Canada Council for the Arts, the Ontario Arts Council (OAC), Ontario Creates, the Government of Ontario, and the Government of Canada for our publishing activities.

for the ones who think nobody sees them
for the ones who don't know that somebody fights for them
for the ones who fight for me
especially
Jesus Fiona Christ, Mom, Kern, Yvette

HOW IT GOES

HOW THE STORY FOUND ME

Belladonna and the Awakening was a chaotic little band in Toronto with Michael Clarke, Johnny Ray Boxcar, Lai Yee Ho, Jeff Burke, Pierre Mongeon, and Kern Albert at the core joined by countless occasional players. The band was not precise, that wasn't the aesthetic. More of a Sun Ra jam band loose-and-lovely feeling aspiring to create what Mikey called "the spirit rising." When we were really cooking Johnny would call for a "face-melting wall of sound." They were good people, good musicians because they shared an innate capacity for listening.

In 2005 we encountered Athletes for Africa (A4A)—Adrian Bradbury and Kieran Hayward. Through them we had heard the story of Uganda's "night commuters." We learned that children in Gulu, Uganda, were walking two and a half hours each night just to sleep under the eye of city lights for fear of abduction into the Lord's Resistance Army. Adrian and Kieran had chosen to replicate this walk themselves in Toronto, making a nightly walk of two and a half hours from Victoria Park Station to City Hall, evoking the journey of these children seeking safety. Others joined them, sleeping on the concrete outside and walking back in the morning before going about their lives. Guluwalk became a movement of international solidarity, with walks occurring in eighty cities across Canada, the USA, Kenya, Serbia, New Zealand, Togo, the UK, China, Australia, Burkina Faso . . .

In those early days, A4A invited bands to station themselves along the route so that walkers would feel encouraged. So we went. We stationed ourselves at the Prince Edward Viaduct Parkette at Castle Frank and watched the crest of the hill as the sky darkened. Suddenly we saw them, the tops of heads resolving into bodies walking steadily towards us, backlit by headlights and street lamps, glowing silhouettes. And suddenly someone shouted, "Play! Play!" and we did, and the dancers danced, and the walkers walked. And then someone said, "We're not done yet!" And someone else was hooking up amps to unknown power supplies loaded into the back of someone's station wagon beside the guitarist and bassist, legs dangling from the tailgate. And the drummer picked up their drums and walked and they handed me a mic, chord snaking through the side window, driving slowly beside us so we could continue to offer our energies all the way down to City Hall.

At the Ontario Coalition for International Cooperation, I met Mercie Blanche Onyut, who worked with women and youth in recovering Gulu. I asked about her work, wondering what could be done. She replied, "God didn't show you this so you could do nothing. You have seen it. What will you do?" I clarified that I had little to offer. I explained that I could dig a hole, or hold a baby while someone else did. She said, "You must come." Okay, yes. I must.

On my first trip to Gulu/Acholiland in 2010, I feared many things, chiefly my limitations. I feared that I would cry (as Jeff D'Hondt had strictly admonished me not to do). I feared that there would be a language barrier. I feared that I was stranded when I arrived in Kampala to learn the flight to Gulu was no longer operating. Three buses later, I entered a village recently relieved of over 140 NGOs who had offered aid at the height of the conflict. The landscape was translated for me by Jimmy Okello, a tireless and compassionate healthcare professional who worked with girl returnees and by Patrick Akera, who offered inroads and security for me to meet with former abductees, former soldiers, young people mapping futures.

Patrick introduced me to the poetry of Okot p'Bitek and helped me to find his books in the local store, alongside other volumes. Among them was a revised teacher-training manual that addressed expectations and strategies for dealing with violence from returned abductees in the classroom. (I write this having recently visited a Montreal classroom where part of the orientation included my first ever Active Shooter Policy. So, that's new . . .

I can tell you about red dirt and the scent of guava plucked from a young tree. I can tell you about maize roasted on the street and motorbike taxis and charismatic churches and a vibrant arts community—including

Dynamo Theatre, who worked with New Harlem to stage *Cake* at the 2011 Bayimba International Festival with Sandra Lefrançois, Neema Bickersteth, Ash Knight, Jeremiah Sparks, and Musa Luswata. Dynamo later collaborated on staging *The Burdens* by Ugandan playwright John Ruganda with director Teddy Nabagonzi at Kendu Hearth, a 2014 theatre conference organized by Mumbi Tindyebwa Otu and Acaye Elizabeth Pamela.

I can tell you about local organizations like YOLRED (Youth Leading Restoration and Development), a group of former abductees who returned, re-rooted in Gulu, and organized to address the specific needs of other returnees. Under the leadership of Geoffrey Omony, their training programs turn out self-sufficient tailors and mechanics, their arts programs hold space for expressive catharsis, while their research partnerships yield essential knowledge in non-extractive interview methods and rural disability access.

I can tell you how my heart nearly burst to welcome poet Otoniya Bitek to our stage, where she spoke of her family, her Ontario life, and her beautiful new book, *A is For Acholi*.

There is so much I could say, about the responsibilities we accept when we convey the experiences of others, about essential truth versus documentary, about big big feelings in the process.

Mostly I'm here to do what I was asked to do by those who shared their stories:

"Tell them what happened here. Tell them we are rebuilding."

DAY 100

by Juliane Okot Bitek

It was the earth that betrayed us first

it was the earth that held onto its beauty
compelling us to return

it was the breezes that were there
& then not there

it was the sun that rose & fell
rose & fell

as if there was nothing different
as if nothing changed

The First Stone was first performed in development at b current theatre's 2008 rock.paper.sistahs festival and the 2008 SummerWorks Festival. The play was first produced by New Harlem Productions and the Great Canadian Theatre Company at Buddies in Bad Times Theatre in Toronto from October 6 to 23, 2022, and in Ottawa from April 11 to 23, 2023, with the following cast and creative team:

Ancestor: Tsholo Khalema
Grandad: Michael-Lamont Lytle
Auntie: Uche Ama
Mom: Dorothy A. Atabong
Girl (Toronto): Makambe K Simamba
| Girl (Ottawa): Nawa Nicole Simon
Boy: daniel jelani ellis
Uma (Toronto): Nawa Nicole Simon
| Uma (Ottawa): Taija Shoné-Chung
Ancestor Echo: Courage Bacchus
Kidogo: Paul Smith
Chorus (Toronto): Taija Shoné-Chung, Gloria Mampuya, Kendelle Parks, Megan Legesse, Tavaree Daniel-Simms, and Willow Martin
| Chorus (Ottawa): Ingrid Gayle, Joy Mwandemange, Kendelle Parks, Megan Legesse, Micah Jondel DeShazer, Oluwakayode Sodunke, and Tifanni Kenny

Director: Yvette Nolan
Assistant Director (Ottawa): Shannon Litzenberger
Production Choreographer: Indrit Kasapi
Associate Choreographer: Pulga Muchochoma
Lighting Design: Michelle Ramsay and Rachel Schaen
Sound Design, Composition, and Choir Director: Maddie Bautista
Associate Sound Design: River Oliveira
Dance Captains: Uche Ama and Kendelle Parks
Projection Design: Cameron Davis
Set Design, Props, and Design Mentor: Jackie Chau

Props Assistant and Design Mentee: Sarah Yuen
Costume Design: Des'ree Gray
Stage Manager: Sarah O'Brien
Assistant Stage Manager: Heather Bellingham
Producer: Alison Wong
Production Manager: Charissa Wilcox
Production Associate: Shanae Sodhi
Chorus Consultant (Toronto) and Chorus Director (Ottawa): Sarah Waisvisz
Nebulous Associate: Lindsay Anne Black

Development of *The First Stone* has been supported by the 2008 Obsidian Theatre Company Playwrights Unit, the Canada Council for the Arts, the Ontario Arts Council, the Toronto Arts Council, the 2013/14 National Arts Centre Playwright Residency, Buddies in Bad Times Theatre, and the 2021 National Creation Fund.

CHARACTERS

Ancestor: ancient, accountable, outside of time
Girl: twelve, female, dutiful, strong
Boy: fourteen, male, inquisitive, resentful
Uma: thirteen, female, open, patient
Mom: thirty-five, female, tired, lonely, resilient
Auntie: forty-five, female, flexible, resourceful, pragmatic
Grandad: fifty-five, male, visionary, obstinate, certain
Kidogo: nine to eleven, a series of child abductees
Chorus: child abductees (voices get younger as the play progresses), children of ancestor (non-verbal but vocal), townsfolk, schoolmates
Father: steadfast, proactive, absent
Baby: passenger, child of Mom and Father
Babygirl: passenger, child of Girl and Grandad
Bushbaby: passenger, abandoned in the bush

SETTING

From the audio description of designer Jackie Chau's set for the premiere production. Future designs need not follow this layout.

At centre stage, beginning at the feet of the front row audience, a shimmery silver river leads towards the back of the stage. At the head of the river is a raised platform with three panels forming a rear wall, over which hangs a thatched grass roof. This is Grandad's house. The area to the right of Grandad's house represents Mom's land, while the area to the left of Grandad's house represents Auntie's land.

When the cast emerges, they will use chalk on the floor, drawing a circle to indicate Mom's house and another to indicate Auntie's house and plants to indicate a garden or field near each home. There is a well located between Grandad's and Auntie's homes. The distance between each home is approximately eight paces.

From the ceiling, twenty feet above, lengths of coloured fabric hang down to the ground, a metre wide. Scattered about are bundles of sticks, patches of tall grass, plastic water canisters, an iron cauldron. At times, a figure appears projected on the panels, the roof, the hanging fabrics, echoing the ancestors' lines in American Sign Language.

OTHERWORDLY

The following terms and figures may be unfamiliar because they are made up:

Opuulyu, Arwa, Orwan: Some of the gods of this land.

Te'mento: A celebratory traditional dance passed down through generations.

Ayehyeh: A facet of call and response, an assurance to the storyteller that the listener is engaged.

PROLOGUE: WHAT THE

ALL sing "The Stone's Ripple."

ALL: Selma, Selma, Selma, ahh, ahh!
Selma, Selma, Selma, ahh, ahh!
I threw the rock that started it all
One hand back so that mine could walk tall
Arwa, Arwa, Arwa
Arwa, Arwa, Arwa
Arwa!

ANCESTOR steps forward and throws a stone into the air, arched towards the darkened stage. We do not hear it land—yet.

ANCESTOR: I am very, impossibly, old.
Not a spirit or a ghost
but a long-gone memory
in the minds of long-dead men.
A vessel for a motion soon to take another host.
Opuulyu.
I am the eyes that saw,
the lips that asked
the ears that learned the answer.
I live on, now, only in the ripples I set off,
still felt as crashing waves ages later.
In the rattle I made,
still heard in deafening echoes after a century.
In the tiny wedge I drove
that took a crack from crevice to chasm.

No one remembers me, really.

No one remembers why it started—
What the first stone was for—
And so no one can think of a reason to stop.

If I had known how much later it would fall,
or how long it would keep on falling,
so that even my great,
great, great *(echoes)*
. . .
Even my descendants would feel it still.

(rising) I threw the rock that started it all.
One arm back so mine could walk tall.
But if I'd only known how hard it would fall
or how many it would fell . . .

The ensemble builds the village playfully. MOM*'s house with a garden and a pot suspended over a fire.* GRANDAD*'s house, central, has beside it a large mortar and pestle.* AUNTIE*'s house is across the river, a distance.*

ALL *sing "The Village Song."*

BOY: Orwan
All we see oh you did make
Orwan
All we give oh you do take

ALL OTHERS: Orwan
All we see oh you did make
Orwan
All we give oh you do take

BOY: Don't curse the gut for its hunger
Don't curse the field for its grain
Don't curse the sky for its thunder
Don't curse the clouds for its rain

ALL OTHERS: Don't curse the gut for its hunger
Don't curse the field for its grain
Don't curse the sky for its thunder
Don't curse the clouds for its rain

BOY: Don't curse the child for its wonder
Don't curse the gourd for its seed
Don't curse the hands for its blunder
Don't curse the sun for its heat

ALL OTHERS: Don't curse the child for its wonder
Don't curse the gourd for its seed
Don't curse the hands for its blunder
Don't curse the sun for its heat

BOY: Orwan give

ALL OTHERS: Orwan take

BOY: Orwan give

ALL OTHERS: Orwan take

BOY: Orwan give

ALL OTHERS: Orwan take

SCENE 1: DOMESTICITY

The stage becomes visible and the rock is heard to echo resoundingly as it clatters down a drainpipe to land between the houses. MOM, AUNTIE, and GRANDAD hear it, peek out of their respective houses, and retreat back inside. Day breaks and MOM rushes BOY and GIRL outside. She hands GIRL a bucket. GIRL and BOY fetch water as she grinds and adds pieces to the pot. En route, BOY pesters GIRL.

GIRL: Stop!

BOY: Baby.

GIRL: Nobody asked you to walk to the well with me.

BOY: You'd probably get scared if I didn't come.

GIRL: No I wouldn't. I did it by myself lots of times.

BOY: You should appreciate my protection. Lots of girls don't have a big brother to take care of them.

GIRL: You mean like Uma?

BOY: Huh?

GIRL: If you're so concerned about my safety, how come you only walk me when I go to the west well?

BOY: Do you want me to follow you everywhere? The east well is close. You're big enough to go there by yourself.

GIRL: Hmm. You know, it's too bad that Uma is so small and weak.

BOY: What are you talking about? She is strong and healthy. She can run faster than you any day.

GIRL: She's very strong.

BOY: Very.

GIRL: Very healthy.

BOY: Very.

GIRL: And yet you help her to raise water and leave the old women to help themselves.

BOY: Why are you always watching me? Are you trying to put God out of a job?

GIRL: Come on.

BOY: I can wait for you here. Hurry up.

GIRL: Just help me. It'll be faster.

BOY sees UMA.

BOY: Hey, wait up. Don't be so impatient.

GIRL begins to draw water. BOY takes the bucket from her and draws water himself, then notices UMA in line behind them and shoves the bucket at GIRL, who stands with it awkwardly throughout their conversation.

Hi.

UMA: Hi.

UMA fills her container.

BOY: So . . .

UMA: So . . .

BOY: Here, let me. That's heavy.

BOY takes the bucket from UMA.

UMA: I thought you might not come here today.

BOY: Of course I came. My sister would get lost if I did not come. The women of our household rely on me while my father is gone.

UMA: What are you staring at?

BOY: Nothing.

UMA: So.

BOY: So. How's school?

UMA: It's good. We're supposed to be getting new books for English. If they come soon I won't have to read *The Magistrate's Hat.*

BOY: I read that last year. It's so long.

Pause.

Do you want to stay and play a while before you go? With my sister.

UMA: I can't. My mother needs me right away, and it's far.

BOY: Let me walk with you. Your neck will get tired and you will have to stop for rest partway and then you will be late and your mother will be angry.

UMA: You can't walk me home.

BOY: I can't?

UMA: No. Your sister is relying on you, remember?

They look at her, shifting their weight.

BOY: She'll be fine.

UMA: Oh, no. Without you to help her neck will get tired and she'll have to stop partway and your mother will be angry.

BOY: Ah ha.

UMA: Anyway, your sister would get lost without you. You had better get her home safely.

BOY: Fine. See you again.

UMA: Goodbye.

(to GIRL) Next time you are going to teach me Te'mento, right?

GIRL: Alright.

BOY: Come on. Stop wasting time.

GIRL and BOY walk home. GRANDAD follows UMA.

GIRL: Can you hold this now?

BOY: Can you be quiet?

GIRL: Did you kiss your girlfriend?

BOY: Did you kiss a yellow frog in the well?

GIRL: Mom, he's bugging me.

MOM: *(holding BABY)* Both of you stop it and help me. You two don't know how lucky you are.

BOY: Yes, by the time we are twenty they will probably have paved a road all the way through town. Then who knows what will come in?

GIRL makes a few sketches of a dance move.

Is that your Te'mento? How are you going to teach Uma something you don't even know?

GIRL: Who are you talking to?

BOY: Your Te'mento is like an old goat trembling.

BOY does an impression of GIRL's dancing.

GIRL: And yours is like a dry tree wilting.

GIRL does an impression of BOY's dancing.

MOM: Ugh. Stop. That is the worst Te'mento I have ever seen. Who taught you that?

GIRL: Show us again, Mom.

MOM: I am busy. I have no time for that.

BOY: Come on, Mom. Show us how it's done.

MOM: Leave an old woman alone.

GIRL: Then I guess this is how we'll do it.

BOY and GIRL continue their exaggeratedly bad dancing.

BOY: How embarrassing. I hope no one from town sees us.

MOM: Stop. Stop it.

Beat.

Okay.

MOM dances reluctantly and then with reserved joy. GIRL and BOY cheer MOM on and then join in, all laughing. The CHORUS joins in the Tèmento.

SCENE 2: SOWING

In the garden outside their home, MOM *pushes seeds into little mounds as* GIRL *watches and pours a little water on each one.*

MOM: Get me that pitcher, Girl. A seed is only small on the outside. Once it's grown it is only what it has become, but when it is small it is still everything it could ever be. It is a small little ball that has so much power in it. But a seed is really only small to the eye and the hand. To the mind and the heart, if you can see it, it is enormous. Nothing is bigger than life, and the potential to create life. If this seed did not need soil to grow, I could show it to you—only for a moment. There is an instant, after it is in the ground, after you have added water—there is a moment when that seed opens—halfway between what it can be and what it will be—there is an opening. And if in that instant you could see into that opening you would see life itself, and neither your eyes, your hand, your heart, or your mind could hold it. So hold it now.

MOM *folds* GIRL*'s hand over the seed and then wraps herself around* GIRL.

GIRL: When will I have a baby of my own to hold?

MOM: Be patient. It will be sooner than you think, but many things must come before a baby.

GIRL: Like what?

MOM: Changes, mostly.

GIRL: Tell me.

MOM: Hm. First, your heart opens wider than it ever has before, to make a place for others to matter more than yourself. Then your eyes will narrow, so that one will fill your vision without blinding you. After that, your belly will grow big until you yourself are two, or three or four, like some women you have heard about. Your breasts become heavy so that you are warmth, shelter, and food at once, and then your back becomes strong so that you can bend and bend without breaking. So that you can put others above you without being crushed.

GIRL: I remember when your belly was this big. Soon afterwards Father went away, you became very tired, and then Baby came.

MOM: And you asked me:

GIRL: "Did we get a new sister because our father is gone?"

MOM: Because you did not yet understand that babies give more than they could ever take away. And / then you held her—

GIRL: Then I held her, and I knew that something so small could not be responsible for Father leaving, or for the bad corn, or the cloudy water, or even for herself.

MOM: You are a very good sister, and you will be a very good mother when it is time. I think that your heart has already become wide. Now you must be patient and wait for the rest. Here, I'll take her while you finish that row.

MOM and GIRL sing.

MOM & GIRL: Grow little seed
When it is dark it will be quiet
So little seed
When there is nothing we will grow again
Nothing ends

SCENE 3: LITTLE BRITCHES

BOY, still playing, picks up and examines a stone with interest.

MOM: This work would go a lot faster if we had some strong men around. Ah, well.

BOY: I'm here, Mom.

MOM: Oh, I don't know. You're so little. Maybe I'll just go ask your grandfather and see if he can help us.

BOY: That old man?

GIRL: He's mean.

BOY: And smelly. I'm strong, Mom. Let me do it.

MOM: Are you sure you wouldn't rather go behind the house and play with your little games, my boy, as a child would do?

BOY: I have no more games. Until my father returns I am the man of the house.

MOM: That is what I thought, and yet when you disrespect Grandfather you speak like a child.

BOY: Do not!

MOM: Those who have travelled the road to manhood have seen the footsteps of their elders and know that someone came before them in order that there may be a road to travel at all.

BOY: I've seen those footsteps; my father's. Big, strong boots with thick treads and tight laces, shined leather with dusted tops. Impossibly new, planting firmly the trunks of his legs, bracing shoulders that filled the doorway and blocked the sun, until he stepped forward, then only his back. My father's form begged to be followed.

BOY stands braced in the doorway and seems to grow. He goes inside.

MOM: If your father were here he would be out here helping me right now.

BOY returns, boots in hand.

BOY: If my father was here a lot of things would be different.

MOM: But he's not, and a lot of things are exactly as they are.

BOY: They are because he is not. How different it could be if he was.

MOM: Would it be so different? This pot would still be as heavy; this fire would be as hot.

BOY: Our crops would have been long planted, our well dug. You would have a husband instead of just being a wife.

MOM: Don't. Your father is a good man. Do you think he has left us? He is gone to protect us.

BOY: So you keep saying. It must be for us, then, that six more children disappeared last night. Six children gone missing from a town that even the spirits feared when my father was at home. Does a lion protect its cubs by leaving the den?

MOM: Who will send money if your father does not go? Who will hold the walls even as they crumble? You should think about things beyond this yard but speak only as far as you know.

BOY: As far as I know . . . I know that I will be like him one day.

MOM: A soldier?

BOY: Gone.

MOM: Your father will be home again when his work is done.

BOY: But he—

MOM: Don't speak about your father anymore.

BOY: You spoke of him. I only answered.

MOM: Well maybe it is best not to answer. Maybe it is best not to respond at all.

BOY: Maybe it is best for a boy to learn from his father how to be a man.

MOM: Such shallow vision will bring you deep trouble.

BOY puts on his father's oversized boots.

Alright, then. You go and pile up that wood over there into the pit, and then you can both fetch kindling.

BOY & GIRL: Alright.

MOM meets AUNTIE at centre. BOY and GIRL begin collecting wood but then GIRL gets a splinter. BOY tenderly removes it. They forget the wood, pick up a game of pebbles stashed behind the house and play. MOM cuts a piece of cane and shares it with AUNTIE. They chew and talk.

MOM: Greetings. I hope that you are well.

AUNTIE: I am as I need to be in order to do what needs to be done.

MOM: As are we all, give thanks.

AUNTIE: Then all is as it should be, and yet you look troubled.

MOM: I was wondering if there is any word.

AUNTIE: They are on the river side of the mountain, sweeping this way, but they will not pass through here.

MOM: So close.

AUNTIE: Your husband sends this.

MOM takes the tobacco pouch offered, giving AUNTIE something small in return.

MOM: Give thanks.

AUNTIE: Your hands are shaking. Is it cold?

MOM: It rains, lately. A hard rain. Pounds so hard it unearths what we have sown. And once exposed, what was yet unborn becomes feed for unscrupulous birds.

AUNTIE: Yes. Those who live off the land will always be troubled by the weather. They will learn to feel changes in the currents of the air, smell rain on the wind, taste tremors in the soil. They will, no doubt, know of these things long before the rest of us, and well prepare.

MOM: Has this rain been coming? Have you seen it coming?

AUNTIE: I have known that in this season the wind carries many ill seeds, and that you must tend your crops closely to keep weeds from taking root. Perhaps in a short time the stalks will be strong enough not to choke, but now, when they are barely shoots, they will not hold their own without your protection.

MOM: Yes.

> *BOY and GIRL hear GRANDAD coming and hide. They take up the stones.*

BOY: You first.

GIRL: No, you.

> *Both throw pebbles at him and run, laughing. GRANDAD catches a stone in mid-air and holds it in his raised fist. He is seen in silhouette, the image of a freedom fighter. As the light returns, he lowers his fist and crushes the stone, pieces crumbling to the ground. BOY and GIRL gather kindling. GRANDAD picks up shards and flings them, contemplates.*

GRANDAD: Lord, I know what it is to have everything taken. You alone know how I have suffered. To have victory snatched from your hands by the lowest of the low, to watch them eat at your table and make love to your wife. To hear them laugh in the face of your destitution. To watch them sip filth from your once-sacred chalice.

BOY: He's going to know it was us.

GIRL: Maybe you. I run like the kudu. He didn't even have a chance to see my heels. You, however, run like moss, so he is probably looking for you right now.

BOY: Oh, you won't be so lucky.

GIRL: Lucky, ha. You don't have to be lucky if you're fast.

BOY: Fast enough to outrun the eyes of a ghost?

GIRL: Ghost. Boys are so schupid. Those are only stories. You shouldn't believe everything you hear.

BOY: I don't.

GRANDAD: I have done everything in my power to fulfill Your vision. You know the multitude who must be pressed into Your service, the sacrifices that must be made, the oppression endured. But the persecution that I bear in Your name is sanctified. Show me Your will in this and all things, and Your word will guide me. Show me the foe and I will slay him with these, Your hands. Show me Your servant and I will grant him shelter. Show me Your true face, oh Lord.

GIRL: You believed Riza was bitten by a poisonous snake.

BOY: I was just being polite. It's rude to call someone a liar right to their face.

GIRL: Sure. What about that old Opuulyu story?

BOY: She saw with eyes we cannot imagine. She heard with inner ears the rumblings behind the rebellion. The spirit called Opuulyu came through her and they saw the wounds of the buffalo and the hippopotamus and learned the reason for this trouble that takes Father to the borders. When Selma came here to speak with Grandfather, everything began. That's not a story, it's history. Mom says—

GIRL: You believe Selma spoke to the mountain?

BOY: And the waterfall.

GIRL: I guess you believe that oil can make you bulletproof, too.

BOY: One bullet has not hit her yet.

GIRL: You're as silly as Grandfather. Three different witches said she didn't have the eye.

BOY: They were lying.

GIRL: Why would they lie?

BOY: Somebody paid them. Even witches have to eat.

GIRL: Whatever.

BOY: Whatever? That's the same as saying I win.

GIRL: Shut up!

GIRL feints towards BOY, who runs around the house. GIRL gathers dropped kindling and brings it to MOM. BOY runs into GRANDAD on the other side.

GRANDAD: You been throwing rocks at my house, Boy?

BOY: No, sir.

GRANDAD: That sound like a question to you? Give me the stone.

BOY shakes his head.

You hear me, Boy? That ain't yours to begin with. Anyone could see it came from my yard. Taking on your father's ways. No good. Now hand it over.

BOY shakes his head.

GRANDAD grabs BOY's arm roughly and pulls him to a crouch beside his sickly field.

You see this? While I was away this gourd became food for a worm and then began to rot, from the inside out. My neighbours must have seen it. They pass here every day, yet it stayed, resting against its brother gourd, and the rot has spread. Now I must plant again, so late in the season, or content myself with what little is left. The rot is spreading. Shall I let it be or shall I root it out?

GRANDAD snaps off the gourd, releasing BOY's arm.

BOY runs away.

Too much like your father. A good bloodline polluted, wasted. Clean water doesn't come from a dirty well. With all that I could give him, he would still be as he is. I once thought that such as he could not be saved, but is it possible that parched ground could come again to life if only I poured on the water of His words?

He licks his fingers and tastes the wind.

We cannot plant anew until we have razed the stubble of last season's harvest. But the people hunger, we have not the time or the men to waste. When we have burnt off these dry stalks they will make way for newer shoots. Even in that ash my new fields will find sustenance. Even within death, there is that which feeds life.

The sound of an airplane overhead. He looks up, points, and then goes into his house. BOY *sees* UMA *hesitating before* GRANDAD*'s house. She remains fixed on the door.*

BOY: Uma . . . did you come to play with my sister?

UMA: No.

BOY: You're very far from home.

UMA: Yes.

BOY: What's wrong?

UMA: Would you help me?

BOY: What?

UMA: If I needed you, would you help me?

BOY: Yes, of course. What's happened?

UMA: My brother is gone.

BOY: Gone where?

UMA: He's gone.

BOY: Where would he go?

UMA: He has run away from home.

BOY: Really?

UMA: No.

BOY: Oh.

BOY and GIRL stare at GRANDAD's house.

UMA: You have heard the same things I have.

BOY: About Arwa?

UMA: Don't be stupid. You know where they go when they are taken.

BOY: Be quiet.

UMA: I'm going to ask Grandad if he has seen my brother.

BOY: I don't think you should—

UMA: Unless you go and ask him for me.

BOY: Uma, you shouldn't be this far from home. Go back to your mother.

UMA: I can't.

BOY: Please. Not today. It's late. Come again tomorrow if your brother hasn't returned.

UMA: It's alright. Go home.

BOY: Uma—

SCENE 4: SHHHHH . . .

MOM is serving out dinner from the pot over the fire.

MOM: You taking your time there, Boy? Come on, now. Before the darkening.

BOY runs back. He and GIRL get a fire going. MOM stirs the pot, ladles dinner into two bowls, and hands them to BOY and GIRL.

There was a girl named Tamani. She was seven. She liked to play by the river and eat honey and listen to the drums. But more than anything she loved secrets. She loved to have them, to keep them and to tell them. One dark night, after everyone was asleep, the ancestors came and whispered to Tamani, "We will tell you a secret if you promise to tell no one." Tamani promised, and they told her a secret. They told her that the well had a loose stone. Tamani did not see why this should be a secret, so she went back to sleep. Give me water.

BOY & GIRL: Ayehyeh. Ayehyeh.

MOM: The next day she told her friend Manu what had happened. Manu promised he would not tell either. That afternoon the king came into town. He announced that he had hidden a golden key somewhere in town in the night, and that whoever found it would be rewarded. Tamani rushed to the well, but the loose stone had already been removed and the golden key taken away. She returned to the town square in time to see Manu receiving his reward. Give me water.

BOY & GIRL: Ayehyeh. Ayehyeh.

CHORUS sings.

CHORUS: Tamani, don't tell nobody

Tamani, don't say a thing

MOM: That night after everyone was asleep the ancestors came and visited Tamani. "You broke your promise, Tamani," they said. "You did not listen. Since you do not listen," they said, "you will not be needing your ears." And with that they chopped off her ears.

BOY and GIRL hear no evil.

CHORUS: Tamani, don't break your promise
Tamani, she promised me

MOM: Tamani cried out, "Please, I promise I will never say anything again." "Is this true?" they asked her. "Oh yes," she said, "I promise." The ancestors smiled and answered, "Since you say will not speak anymore, you will not be needing your lips," and with that they chopped off her lips.

A cry rips through the night—UMA.

BOY and GIRL speak no evil.

After that, everyone told their secrets to Tamani, because she had become very good at keeping them.

CHORUS: Tamani, don't tell nobody
Tamani, don't say a thing
Tamani, don't break your promise
Tamani, she promised me

Hush, Tamani, hush, Tamani, hush, Tamani, hush, Tamani, hush, Tamani, hush, Tamani, hush, Tamani, hush, Tamani

MOM sees no evil.

MOM: Now into bed, you two. You know how the spirits like to find you awake so they can feast on the energy you're supposed to be saving for tomorrow—and the two of you fat and well-fed, tonight, too. Better close those eyes.

BOY and GIRL go into the house. MOM stokes coals to smoulder overnight and goes into the house. GRANDAD is vaguely seen creeping to the window and trying the latch. He cuts the screen on the window.

BOY: Mom?

MOM: Ask Orwan to watch over you and go back to sleep.

GRANDAD stops cutting and leaves.

BOY: Mom, is Arwa stronger than Orwan?

MOM: Go to sleep.

BOY: Because he has a whole ghost army, right? What does Orwan have?

MOM: He has anything he wants. Go to sleep.

MOM notices the screen.

Come on, kids, get up and fetch me some water.

GIRL: I'll go!

MOM: No, I want you to go together today—and not all the way to the west well. Stay close today.

GIRL: But the east well water makes the rice smell.

BOY: Don't argue. Just stay close to me. Let's go. Come on. I will show you how to choose a good walking stick.

BOY and GIRL exit.

MOM approaches GRANDAD's house with tea.

MOM: Grandad, can I bring you some tea?

There is no answer.

Grandfather, did you hear anything near the house last night?

GRANDAD emerges from the house, takes the cup, and drinks.

GRANDAD: I hear things every night. I hear how close we are to paradise on earth. I hear the pitter patter of little feet. I hear . . . change on the wind. I am patient.

MOM: It's good to know that you are close by, should there be trouble. I know that you care for my children, and the others, as though they were your own.

GRANDAD: We are all precious in His eyes, my dear. We are all born to be of service to Him, in whichever way He chooses.

MOM: Of course.

GRANDAD: Perhaps when your husband returns things will be better.

MOM: My husband is where he must be.

GRANDAD: Is he?

MOM: He is serving—

GRANDAD: Who does he serve? There is only One who is worth serving. You would do well to remember that. It is only through His power that we are powerful. It is only through His wisdom that we are wise. Think on this and you will see that it is so. Even those who claim to serve Him pervert His will. So many are impure; so few can see.

MOM: We planted today.

GRANDAD: That's good.

MOM: A bit late in the season but the soil is good. Good enough.

GRANDAD: Yes.

MOM: The children—

GRANDAD: You should go to the children.

MOM: Yes. The night has become so restless, Grandfather. It makes one anxious.

GRANDAD drinks the last, grunts, and hands MOM the empty cup. She goes back to her house.

GRANDAD: For lo, He speaks in many tongues

I heard one such last night but one
An echo of forgotten sons
Or of forgotten sins

Take for Him that which is His
Use all that He graciously gives
Make “what was” into “what is”
and thereby live.

GRANDAD *dons the military fancies of a general to the echoes of the rock tumbling down the drainpipe.*

SCENE 5: CHATTY

BOY and GIRL emerge from behind the house. BOY is sullen.

GIRL: Hey.

BOY shrugs.

Hey, maybe we can go to the west well tomorrow.

BOY: I don't care.

GIRL: Uma says she is going to—

BOY: She'll be at the east well.

GIRL: Oh, good. That pitcher is nearly empty. We'll have to go soon.

BOY: Have you seen her?

GIRL: Yes, I see her all the time. Why? You want to know if she asked about you?

BOY: Did you see her yesterday?

GIRL: No, I— What? Did I see what?

BOY: *(over his shoulder)* I don't want you to go to the well anymore.

GIRL: Are you afraid I'll say something to your girlfriend? Stop trying to boss me.

BOY: Listen to me. You should not try to be so smart. Some stories are more real than you think. Uma is—I think Uma has been telling somebody's secrets.

GIRL: Why are you saying that? I saw her only last week.

BOY: And I saw her yesterday, although she took care to pass by late when the light was fading. You will not see her there in the daytime anymore.

GIRL covers her mouth with both of her hands. BOY covers his ears.

Maybe she didn't think about what she was saying. Maybe she didn't believe that anyone was listening. Now will you be more cautious?

GIRL: What terrible person would—

BOY: Aren't you listening to me? Be more careful with your words. You may laugh when I speak of Arwa, but someone is listening.

GIRL: *(whispering)* What did she tell you?

BOY: I did not speak to her, and neither should you.

GIRL: She's done nothing to deserve that.

BOY: Do you think such things happen to blameless people? Even nothing may be something. You may be condemned for your stillness as much as for your actions. Who knows what offence we may already have committed in another's eyes? Be careful, be quiet, and do as I say.

MOM emerges and they all tend the garden silently.

MOM: Lucky you went right to sleep last night. I thought I heard Arwa creeping around, looking for healthy ones like you two.

GIRL: Oh stop, Mom. What does a great god of war want with a little girl?

BOY: I heard it, too.

MOM: If you heard something it wasn't Arwa. If it had been, and he'd found you awake, you wouldn't be here now.

BOY: No, it wasn't Arwa. I think it was Grandad.

BOY pulls a stone from his pocket.

Mom, is this rock something special?

MOM: *(takes it thoughtfully)* No, not special, just old. Very old. Too old. It should be long ground into dust.

She pockets the stone.

GIRL: Mom, what happened to—

BOY: Tell me about my father's gun.

MOM: Why should you want to know about his gun?

GIRL: Because he's a boy.

BOY shoots GIRL coolly with a pointed finger because he's a boy.

Mom!

MOM: Watch where you're pointing that.

GIRL: Tell us about his uniform.

MOM: Alright, it has two stripes right here, and he wears his hat just so, like this, to say, "I am one of you, brothers, and also very much my own man." His green pants are tucked tightly into the tops of his shiny black boots, his shirt into his pants and he is all angles, crisp, and when he moves in the night it is just like the jungle, shifting. When he moves at night, from what I can remember, he is both silent and strong. And now I will tell you about—

BOY: His gun. Tell us.

MOM: Okay . . . Your father's new gun is a rifle, like any other. The barrel is as long as your arm, hollow like a pipe, straight as his back and black as his face.

BOY: His new gun is bigger than his old gun. With a gun like that everyone will fear and respect him. With a gun like that you could do anything.

MOM: Listen to me. A gun is not like a knife, which can cut flesh from a carcass or choking weeds from a stalk. A knife can be used in many ways. A gun is a tool, made for only one thing, and that is to kill.

BOY: It's darkening. I'll feed the fire.

MOM: No! You and your sister are sleeping at Auntie's tonight. Go get what you need.

GIRL: Mom, it's late. That's three hours away.

MOM: Best go quickly, then.

BOY and GIRL go into the house and return with packs.

Quickly and quietly. Go now.

GIRL: You're not coming?

MOM hands BABY to GIRL.

MOM: Go.

CHORUS: Quick, quiet, quick, quiet, feet don't fail me
Quick, quiet, quick, quiet, feet don't fail me
Quick, quiet, quick, quiet, feet don't fail me

BOY and GIRL run towards AUNTIE's house as it darkens. A light goes on in GRANDAD's house as they pass. AUNTIE welcomes them expectantly.

AUNTIE: Come. Quickly. Quietly.

BOY, GIRL, and AUNTIE go inside AUNTIE's house. Shots ring out. Small footsteps scamper in the night. MOM waits in the yard, stoking the small fire. GRANDAD enters. MOM approaches him with tea, which he does not take from her.

The "Feet Don't Fail Me" underscore begins quietly among the children.

MOM: It's late, Grandad.

GRANDAD: Yes, it is.

MOM: Too late to be out, don't you think?

GRANDAD: Best to go in then.

MOM: Arwa's been about. Lots of kids go missing in the night.

GRANDAD: Yes, the police should be offering better protection. You should make them aware of your displeasure with the quality of their service.

MOM: I worry that he will come for mine. I hope they are safe.

GRANDAD: *(smiling)* He only comes for those who are born to go to Him. I hope that yours are safe, too.

MOM: Are they, do you think?

GRANDAD: Best to get inside now. Good night.

> *GRANDAD merges with the darkness. His heavy footsteps are heard amid the small scampers.*

MOM: Good night, Grandad.

> *MOM goes home. At each corner of their property she chews two leaves, gestures, and lays them down for protection. GRANDAD may not cross this line anymore.*

SCENE 6: CONSCRIPTION

AUNTIE comes out of her house and hands BABY to a sleepy BOY and GIRL, urging them with signs to get moving.

AUNTIE: Go now. Quickly and quietly.

GIRL: Quickly.

BOY: Quietly.

AUNTIE: Go.

GIRL: Quickly.

BOY: Quietly.

AUNTIE: Go.

CHORUS begins singing "Prayer of the Gun."

CHORUS: This stone is a bone caught in the throat of a memory . . .

GIRL: Quickly.

BOY: Quietly

GRANDAD: Come here.

GIRL: Quickly . . .

CHORUS: This stone is a bone
Caught in the throat
Of a memory
A hole
At the bottom of the boat
Leaving real men to drown
And fables to float.

BOY is taken by the children. GIRL gets home. GRANDAD and BOY are seen in silhouette. MOM takes GIRL and BABY inside.

MOM: This stone . . .

AUNTIE: This stone is a bone
Caught in the throat
Of a memory
A hole
At the bottom of the boat
Leaving real men to drown
And fables to float
Or fables to feed.

MOM begins tending the small shoots in the garden.

GIRL: Shall I go get water?

MOM: No. We'll make do with what we have. Give me that pitcher.

GIRL: I heard things last night.

MOM: Best for you to use your nights for sleep. Sleeping during the day gives you short legs, you know.

GIRL: There are worse things.

MOM: You, Girl, you be good. There will be good things for you.

MOM corrects GIRL's handling of a shoot.

Gently. Small things will make big worries until they grow.

GIRL: Is he with them, in the woods?

MOM: I think so.

GIRL: Will he come back?

MOM: Get your things together, now. I'll give you soup before you go.

GIRL goes into the house. MOM ladles soup into a bowl. GIRL re-enters, drinks the soup, and hands back the bowl.

Quickly and quietly. Go.

MOM hands BABY to GIRL. She runs to AUNTIE's house where she is welcomed by AUNTIE. Small footsteps scamper by. A great barrage of gunfire is heard.

SCENE 7: HARDENED

GRANDAD oversees the tired children.

GRANDAD: Why are you moving so slowly?

BOY: It is their feet. The grass is cutting. They need shoes.

GRANDAD: Let me see. Yes, this is bad. We cannot go on so slowly.

BOY: Will we stop?

GRANDAD: Yes. Bring all the children. Lay down with your heads facing west. Now, cut the bottoms of their feet like this.

BOY: How will they walk?

GRANDAD: They won't walk.

BOY: Oh, good. I thought—

GRANDAD: It is soon time to run. They will run. They will heal, they will harden, they will not slow down again.

BOY: Yes, sir.

GRANDAD and the children sing "Give Me Water/Feet Don't Fail Me."

CHILDREN: Give me water
Give me water
Make me for one thing only
Give me water
Give me water
Make me for one thing only
Give me water
Give me water
Make me for one thing only

Quick, quiet, quick, quiet, feet
Don't fail me
Quick, quiet, quick, quiet, feet
Don't fail me
Quick, quiet, quick, quiet, feet
Don't fail me

GRANDAD: No rest, just fight
For days, for nights
No eat, no bite
No rest, just fight
For days, for nights
No eat, no bite
No rest, just fight
For days, for nights
No eat, no bite

CHILDREN: Cut my feet, crush my head
Sweat my tears, bleed my bread
Cut my feet, crush my head
Sweat my tears, bleed my bread
Cut my feet, crush my head
Sweat my tears, bleed my bread

SCENE 8: SETBACK

GRANDAD accepts tea from AUNTIE.

GRANDAD: Good morning, Auntie.

AUNTIE: I heard much rain in the night. I was afraid your food might have washed away.

GRANDAD: Not mine, but His.

AUNTIE: As are they.

GRANDAD: And therefore made well for His purpose. Young, strong, worthy.

AUNTIE: Mm. How young is too young, Grandfather? Even a child can hold and aim a rifle. Does that mean they were made for it?

A long silence as GRANDAD considers this.

GRANDAD: Thank you for bringing this.

GRANDAD gives her an offering in return.

AUNTIE: We are one stomach. If you starve, how will I survive?

GRANDAD: Mm.

AUNTIE: Grandad, the ache goes on so long I worry that we are slowly bleeding out. I wonder whether your patience is serving us now. The people still believe . . .

GRANDAD: Our work goes well.

AUNTIE: Yes. Grandfather, crops are being burned. Plots trampled. The people . . . the people believe but . . . faith is . . . strengthened by acts of benevolence.

GRANDAD: True faith needs no sign. Does yours falter?

AUNTIE: Not mine, no.

GRANDAD: It seems people have less to offer us lately.

AUNTIE: Dry season.

GRANDAD: Or perhaps a portion has been offered elsewhere. To feed the enemy is an act of treason, and our opponents have been looking too fat for field rations. Auntie, when we pass through the village tomorrow, no crops will be burned and no homes disturbed.

AUNTIE: Thank you.

GRANDAD: Because what we need will be prepared for us and delivered to the church steps.

AUNTIE: Thank you. You are benevolent.

GRANDAD: Good day, Auntie.

AUNTIE leaves.

Our ranks are depleted. Our stores run down to only crumbs. Your children eat stalks in the absence of fruit and await the future I have promised them, the future they fight for, although many will never see it dawn.

I will prove worthy of this test. I will take Your people and climb from this low place to the height of Your glory so that all will know the true power of our faith by our survival. You have brought us low to show that even Your lowliest are made to be of use and I have heard. We shall not be herded from ancestral lands; we shall not be ended; we shall not be forgotten.

We are all one, Lord, and I am remiss in my blindness to your many gifts, for the simple stone can be made into a blade, and the branch into a shaft. The patience I have prized is an affront to the urgency of your work. Your day draws near and I will make haste to be ready. We must all be swifter, stronger, and more resolute. Thank you for your guidance in this and all things.

GRANDAD addresses the soldiers, holding two identical seeds.

Tell me, which of these is greater?

He awaits an answer.

You see, it is not only Tumi here who is blind. Heh. Eh, Tumi? I do not think you will be caught daydreaming again! But you are not the only blind one here. We, all of us, fail to see. Only God can count the number of fruits in a single seed. This is why we must plant each one and see what comes by His grace.

Bring me the little ones. Let us see how well He has made them.

SCENE 9: ALL THE KING'S HORSES

GIRL prepares to run to safety with BABY. BOY and GRANDAD prepare to snatch her.

GIRL: Shhhhhh. By the time you are old enough to run you won't have to.

GRANDAD: Go on. Remember what I have told you. She is not your sister but His warrior.

BOY: Yes.

GIRL: Boy.

BOY: Come here.

GRANDAD: Very good. You can sleep inside tonight.

BABY cries.

You, Girl, put the baby down.

GRANDAD points to the grinding apparatus and GIRL lays BABY in the mortar. GRANDAD hands her the pestle.

You've done this before.

GIRL: I can't.

BOY: Quickly.

GIRL: Quickly . . . quietly.

> *GIRL begins grinding. She grinds with increasing intensity, smiling as she does so. At last the crying ceases.*

MOM: Oh . . .

GRANDAD: You have done well. Come inside.

> *GRANDAD puts his jacket over GIRL's shoulders and strokes her head affectionately. GIRL laughs abruptly, hysterically.*

You see, children? Here is a soldier who can find joy in her work. Look well on her.

SCENE 10: ENOUGH ALREADY

MOM comes out and crosses to AUNTIE's house. The children clumsily execute military training choreography.

MOM: Auntie, did my girl leave here this morning?

AUNTIE: She did. Didn't she—

MOM: She hasn't arrived. And the baby . . .

AUNTIE: Two of them.

MOM: Three. All. How can this be?

AUNTIE: It just is. The soldiers are advancing. They have reached the valley west of town.

MOM: So close. Is this a good thing?

AUNTIE: What is good? They advance now because more than half of Grandad's army were killed in the night. More than half.

MOM: So what do I hope for? What should we want? My husband is gone, fighting. My children sent to take his bullets.

AUNTIE: And whose children took his bullets last week?

MOM: What can be done?

AUNTIE: They have all been made into killers now. What can be done?

MOM: They should hang.

AUNTIE: Is that what you want?

MOM: I want my children to come home.

AUNTIE: At what cost?

MOM: Any. I just want them to come home and be my children again.

MOM goes home and removes the leaves she has placed for the kids' protection.

Till, sow, (dig), grow.

Weed. Water. Wait. Wait.
Light the fire
Beasts, birds, pests, drought
Snatch, tangle, wrench out
Come dinnertime there's nothing left
To put into the pot
And I have to give something
So I begin to tear little pieces of myself
Pieces of me pressed
Between the heat below
And the (weight) above
You wouldn't think I would feel it
But I can feel every piece of me
That has ever been
Touched, torn or taken
No matter how far
I can feel every piece of me.

The CHORUS continues its military choreography, singing "Prayer of the Gun."

CHORUS: This stone is a bone
Caught in the throat
Of a memory
A hole
At the bottom of the boat
Leaving real men to drown
And fables to float
Fables to float.

SCENE 11: KIDOGO

AUNTIE visits GRANDAD in the woods where they have made camp.

AUNTIE: It is getting hard to find shelter. Tall trees fall all around us.

GRANDAD: Those who are useful will survive.

AUNTIE: I am too old to fight beside you, but I can still be of use. I have eyes and ears. I see much.

GRANDAD: He welcomes all offers of service.

AUNTIE: I imagine the youngest of them must be a burden to you.

GRANDAD: Even our burdens are blessings in that they strengthen us for greater weights to come.

AUNTIE: My burden feels light compared with yours. Are there any who weigh you down? Any that you have no use for?

GRANDAD: No use?

AUNTIE: Grandfather, you must dream of them one day going home, else why defend their homeland?

GRANDAD: You grow impatient.

GRANDAD gestures a command to the children. He goes into the house and brings out GIRL. At his gesture, GIRL holds out BABY's blanket. AUNTIE takes it.

I have no use for this one. Take it.

AUNTIE: Thank you. I offer you this maize and millet. Your army is growing, and growing . . . soldiers . . . must be fed.

GRANDAD gestures and GIRL takes the offering inside. AUNTIE leaves. GRANDAD marshals troops. One small boy is slow to line up.

GRANDAD: Kidogo, what is wrong?

KIDOGO: Nothing.

GRANDAD: You can tell me.

KIDOGO: We have been running all day and all night.

BOY: Please, he's only six.

GRANDAD: Shh. Let the child tell me what is wrong.

BOY: He is fine.

KIDOGO: I am tired.

GRANDAD: Oh no! That is no good. Do you want to take a rest?

KIDOGO: Yes, please.

GRANDAD abruptly draws a gun and shoots KIDOGO in the head.

GRANDAD: There. Now you can rest all you like. Is anyone else tired?

The CHILDREN *resume military choreography with growing proficiency, singing "Prayer of the Gun."*

CHILDREN: Stone into blade, branches to shaft
Make me for one thing only, oh Arwa
Stone into blade, branches to shaft
Make me for one thing only, oh Arwa
Stone into blade, branches to shaft
Make me for one thing only. Ayeyeh

SCENE 12: HARDER

AUNTIE emerges from the shadows with an armful of BUSHBABY, with other implied children staying back in the shadows. She hesitates to come to MOM, who hesitates to be hopeful.

MOM: Auntie, will you bless my house today by entering?

AUNTIE: Not today, thank you. I have a long way to go before nightfall, and many stops on the way.

MOM: What have you brought?

AUNTIE: Don't get your hopes up. I don't have—

MOM lunges at BUSHBABY.

MOM: Baby? Baby?! This isn't / Baby.

AUNTIE: No, I'm / sorry.

MOM: I don't know this / child!

AUNTIE: Are you sure? Please look closer. Don't you recognize this nose? Are these eyes familiar? A neighbour, maybe?

MOM: No, they're not familiar. Should they be? Who is her mother?

AUNTIE: I don't know.

MOM: Where did she come from?

AUNTIE: Bush. These were left behind when they moved on. I want to bring them home to their grandmothers, if I can. But no one recognizes them. Not yet.

MOM: I'm sorry. I don't see my girl in this face.

AUNTIE: Alright. Maybe the next village will know her. I'd better go.

MOM: Yes, someone will want them.

AUNTIE: Maybe.

AUNTIE starts to leave but turns back.

Mother, the last time we spoke you said you would do anything. I have come to speak again, in more realistic terms. This is real life. There is no everything, nothing, anything. Absolutes are for poetry. In this place, we have only some, few, and many.

MOM: No, we still have nothing. There is nothing I would not do.

AUNTIE: Except what you cannot. Don't be hasty. Understand what I am asking. If they return, can you look at them without seeing the baby you have lost at their hands? When they won't laugh it will break you. When they cry it will tear you open.

MOM: I am a mother. I'm strong because I have to be. For their sake I have done things I would never dream of doing for myself. How can you understand? They are my children.

AUNTIE: When you find that you no longer know them, will they still be yours?

MOM: Were they ever mine?

AUNTIE: Only to care for.

MOM: Only to care for.

AUNTIE: You will look at them and see your failure; you will fear them and forget to love them. They will be strangers in your home. Killers.

MOM: Children.

AUNTIE: No. You can guess at what they've seen, what they have done. You cannot imagine what they are thinking, what shape the shadows take in their dreams. They are not young anymore, only small.

MOM: You speak of them only as they are now. Time will soften them towards me.

AUNTIE: Or harden you towards them.

MOM: Do you want me to give up my children?

AUNTIE: No, only to know what they are, and to know yourself because if they come home and you are not prepared you will regret it.

MOM: You've seen them.

AUNTIE: No, others like them.

MOM: How did they—

AUNTIE: You can't bring them here! They are worse than animals! After what they have done, there is no going back. No healing. Better to be dead than what they are now. You say you are a mother and yet you did not protect them. Your husband abandoned your home. Why should we continue to suffer? Why should we pile this new misery upon our grief?

MOM: Stop! How can you say these things? You, who have no children, who have never given blood for another's life. They are mine. I failed them but they are mine.

She weeps.

AUNTIE: Mother, is this your strength? The people in town will say these things and more to you. What will you do, scream? Cry each time you are challenged? You will soon grow tired and ashamed if you aren't already. Useless. This is why I ask you to consider, and to know yourself.

MOM: What if—

AUNTIE: What if they come home, as I have said. Grandfather, too, will come home. Do you understand what you are agreeing to?

MOM: That old man . . .

AUNTIE: Lives a stone's throw away. One day he will come to your door. He will ask you to pour him tea. He will eat from your pot and take your hand in his, pat your son on the head, and lift your daughter onto his knee as if . . .

MOM: As if . . .

AUNTIE: As if she were his own.

MOM: She isn't.

AUNTIE: She is now.

MOM: What do you want from me?

AUNTIE: Can you forgive Grandad? I know this is a very hard thing I am asking.

MOM: Nothing is harder than this. If he will let them come home, I will welcome him—even that.

AUNTIE: Can you speak for Father? Will he too welcome them, whatever they've become?

MOM: He will. Everything he does is to bring our children home.

AUNTIE: Those who can still return . . . What was her name?

MOM: Baby.

AUNTIE: It is a beautiful name. I will speak to him.

MOM: He won't speak to you. He speaks to no one, only preaches.

AUNTIE: This is true, but me? He has known me for a long time, since before the Lord first rattled in his ear. If you say you will forgive him, let me try. He knows that your husband is returning soon and will want an accounting. He must see the place he has put himself.

MOM: I'm grateful. Whatever the outcome. I doubt that you will move him, but I pray that you can.

AUNTIE: I will have to take an offering.

MOM: Of course.

MOM gives AUNTIE a large offering.

AUNTIE: Go now. You can do no good by neglecting the crop.

MOM leaves. AUNTIE turns to ANCESTOR.

Ancestor, I live in your legacy. Is this what you envisioned? Was I intended to do something different? To offer them to you more willingly?

AUNTIE is overloaded. She calculates her capacity and decides to leave BUSHBABY behind, lowering them into the river. ANCESTOR buoys BUSHBABY, who fusses. UMA emerges from the shadows and lifts BUSHBABY from the river: an adoption.

SCENE 13: NEW HAT

Bush.

GRANDAD: Okay, time to move.

KIDOGO: The food is cooking.

GRANDAD: Bring it.

KIDOGO: From the fire? How shall I?

GRANDAD: Where is your hat?

KIDOGO: My what?

GRANDAD: Oh, here it is. You've been cooking beans in it.

GRANDAD picks up the still bubbling pot.

Get me some leaves and rope. Kidogo has gotten a new hat.

The boiling pot is tied to the child's head with a thin layer of leaves to protect his head. KIDOGO squirms in discomfort.

Show the boys your hat. Why are you so jumpy? Discipline, soldier. Stand still so they can get a good look at it. Now, boys, it seems some of the villagers have been giving food to our opposition. Is that loyalty? Is it gratitude? Is betrayal to go unanswered? Let them scurry from their homes into the high grasses with other vermin and tremble there.

The children pack the remains of camp quickly and prepare for a raid on the village. They sing "Run to the Fields."

CHILDREN: Long time ago, weyo weyo
We run in the field, play-o play-o
New Papa come and so and so
We run to the field, weyo weyo.
Run to the field, weyo-o
Run to the fields we say-o say
Go run to the fields
Weyo, weyo, weyo

SCENE 14: GOOD WORKS

MOM goes home and tends to grown plants while AUNTIE brings tea to GRANDAD. At first BOY and GIRL, stationed outside his door, stop her. BOY sticks his head in the door and GRANDAD soon emerges.

GRANDAD: Perhaps today you will die, eh?

GRANDAD hugs them both roughly.

Ha ha. No, little ones. Today there is still much to do. Much to make pure.

He takes a melon from inside the house and throws it to the ground near the pestle, yelling.

BOY and GIRL fall upon the melon with sticks and savagely beat it through the next scene. AUNTIE approaches and GRANDAD leaves his supervision of the children to speak with her, taking the tea.

Auntie, you honour me in coming here. Do you come to marvel at the Lord's good works?

AUNTIE: Yes.

GRANDAD: Mm. I thought you came to bring me advice. So many people with helpful suggestions lately.

AUNTIE: Father had hoped to speak with you.

GRANDAD: Then let him come and say so for himself.

AUNTIE: Your men will not let him pass.

GRANDAD: Hmm. What can be done?

AUNTIE: Now I have come to speak with you, Grandfather.

GRANDAD: So many who seek my ear these days, in this place and the next. So many suggestions. So many voices hoping to drown Him out, but I am always listening.

AUNTIE: Does He still speak to you, Grandad? Or is the voice you hear your own?

GRANDAD: You mistake my welcome for liberty. Why have you come here?

AUNTIE: Grandfather, I fear Arwa has become insatiable.

GRANDAD: He only takes those He needs for His work, and His work is for us all, so we should all be glad to serve.

AUNTIE: And yet those who go are younger and younger all the time. It is hard to believe that ones so young . . .

GRANDAD: There are some as young as these in Father's camp. What is it about mine that offends you? Is it the fit of their uniforms?

AUNTIE: Father is not blameless. But surely a divine spirit inspires more mercy than a man.

GRANDAD: It is senseless to spare a life today that will be taken tomorrow if by the use of that life today you can save ten.

AUNTIE: But this way is beyond all reason.

GRANDAD: Do you expect to reason with a spirit?

AUNTIE: Only if he is a spirit who can see the inevitable, hear the mountain crumbling above him, and seek to step aside. Despite all that has happened, all that people say . . . I know this spirit is righteous. If he has become trapped here well beyond his intended time, he may be grateful for an escape from what he has begun—an end to this, which will leave all as it was. You must be so tired, Grandfather.

GRANDAD: So much running. What can be done? Look at how easily she swings the machete. That one is good at many things. One of our best.

AUNTIE cuts cane and shares it. They chew.

AUNTIE: The people are afraid.

GRANDAD: That is why I fight for them. The soldiers oppress them and starve them, keeping out the roads, the money. Force us into the corners of our own land—

AUNTIE: The people are afraid of you.

GRANDAD: Only those who know their hearts to be unclean need fear me.

AUNTIE: And who is safe?

GRANDAD: Why do you people push against me, even while I pour out my blood for you?

AUNTIE: For who? Who is left?

GRANDAD: I have sacrificed—

AUNTIE: Yes, you have. Once you have sacrificed everyone, who will be saved?

GRANDAD chews.

The soldiers have begun paving that road. They stand in the sun beside the workers, and their features are a smudge in the heat. There is one who wears his hat just so. He is all angles, strong. He carries a gun as long as your arm and as black as his face. He is looking for his son.

GRANDAD: I will not be pardoned if I send them home.

AUNTIE: Nor if you keep them here.

GRANDAD: I won't retreat. I won't hide.

AUNTIE: And yet the Lord Himself rested. There's word you may be called upon up north. What then? Surely you won't travel that distance with all of them?

GRANDAD: I won't be made a villain.

AUNTIE: A hero, Grandfather. It is because of you they are alive now and not corrupted by our conquerors.

GRANDAD: Not a day in prison. Not one word of recrimination.

AUNTIE: Silence.

GRANDAD: And our soldiers.

AUNTIE: Our soldiers?

GRANDAD: They must be kept well. If they are needed again—

AUNTIE: I understand.

GRANDAD: It has been hard to hear His voice in all this noise. A man cannot stand under fire and lay down his arms. A people cannot subside, cease to be what they are. We have been hunted, spilled from one land into another, despised for sins that are not our own. Should I lay down now? Let them come for me? For all of us?

AUNTIE: Father, too, wants to come home. Everybody wants to go home. It is time. Time for you to walk in the streets among your people, to sleep in your own bed, to return. A hero . . .

MOM sings "Bring My Babies Home."

MOM: All day, all night alone
Bring my babies home
Pray for the day I can hold my own
Bring my babies home
All this time, they must be grown
Bring my babies home
It's been so long, whoa-o
It's been so long, whoa-o

SCENE 15: SCATTERED

AUNTIE approaches MOM with BOY and pregnant GIRL and BABY's blanket.

MOM: Why don't you go inside the house now?

BOY and GIRL go in.

AUNTIE: Remember what you've said.

MOM: What do you mean?

GRANDAD: Good afternoon.

AUNTIE: Good afternoon, Grandad.

GRANDAD: The crops are coming up nicely. Where are the children?

AUNTIE: In the house.

GRANDAD: Don't they know that sleeping during the day makes short legs?

AUNTIE grips MOM by the shoulders.

AUNTIE: We shouldn't hold you back . . . Grandad.

GRANDAD: Yes, I'm expected in town.

He takes a last look at the crop.

Those ones on the edge look bruised. You should be careful. Might be best to cut them down now, save trouble later.

He leaves.

MOM: Oh. I was just going to take the children into town. Maybe we'll go later.

AUNTIE: Mother, people are saying things.

MOM: Noise. People make noise whether or not the sound has meaning. We're so like birds that way.

AUNTIE: Easily scattered. Frightened.

MOM: We're that, too.

AUNTIE: It would be better if the people in town did not see Boy and Girl very often. They're afraid.

MOM: And me? I've done nothing.

AUNTIE: You harbour them. Many people feel that isolation may be the best thing for them right now. While they recover.

MOM: I understand, but this is our home. Should I keep them inside at all hours? What can be done?

AUNTIE: What can be done? Hmmm. Let us spend the night thinking about it and speak again tomorrow. Your children are home. Give them their dinner and love them.

AUNTIE goes around the perimeter of the property biting and laying leaves from the outside with a gesture to keep the children in. Night falls. People come with fire.

PEOPLE: Animals. / Murderers. / Where is my husband? / Have you seen my son? / Filth.

BOY: Whore.

GIRL: Coward.

MOM: No!

AUNTIE: Hm.

GRANDAD whistles.

PEOPLE: Savages. / Killers. / Why did you come here? / Where is my daughter? / Burn.

MOM: Get out of the house. Quickly. Quietly. Come.

They run from the house as it comes apart. The people rage.

PEOPLE: Strike rot!
Strike rot
Strike rot
Strike rot
Strike rot
Strike rot
Strike rot
Strike rot

INTERLUDE: SERIOUSLY

ANCESTOR builds a little pile of stones.

ANCESTOR: Legacy bleeds until names are blurred,
the landslide obscured by the mud.
The legend veiled by living blood.
Arwa.
My hands, once cradle of a nation,
have grown too heavy to mould this gravel
back into the mountain from whence it came.
That mass that moved me as I shook it,
unbound, unbidden, assumes a coarser shape,
unheld, unhealed,
forever to bear these rifts and scars
as testament.
Whether to salvage or to shame
remains unwritten,
but the scribe's hand advances with our every breath,
and there is only one way: forward.

Once the fall is manifest,
the rolling stone does come to rest.
Now drifts the dust we did ingest
or did unjust.

SCENE 16: LAZY

IDP camp. A blanket-stick-tent approximation of their previous home. MOM carries GIRL's BABYGIRL. GIRL stares into the distance.

GIRL: What have I done? My eyes won't see.
This arm, this hand's no part of me.
There is no safe place to be.
Mercy. Mercy. Mercy.

MOM: She is fresh; a blossom of untried being. Still smart enough to / love everyone, touch everything, trust . . . Eyes so clear, go right through me, finding the love I had pressed between pages. Nothing to do with "now," but here again. She breathes and needs and . . . cries and bleeds and . . . She is an echo of a grief I cannot relieve and freely relive.

BABYGIRL cries. MOM takes her to GIRL and positions BABYGIRL to breastfeed while GIRL looks away.

GIRL: She cries, a pin sticking her or she's hungry. I don't know, but she is not afraid. She doesn't know fear yet. I put her down. The wood at the bottom is round and smooth from grinding. She doesn't know what is in my hand, on my face, in my heart. She doesn't know anything, only that it is getting darker. A crescent of light is closing. I won't scream because she doesn't have to know. I smile for her and think to myself, "Hurry! Doing it slowly is worse." And I try to grind faster. Then it is quiet. Every time she cries, I think it is going to get dark again.

MOM: It's time to get water.

BOY sits.

GIRL helps.

The fire needs wood.

BOY drinks.

GIRL helps.

This pot is very heavy.

BOY watches.

GIRL helps.

I'm tired. *(nothing)* I think I'll just rest awhile before I . . .

MOM goes inside. BOY shuffles cards.

BOY: Do you remember Josiah? Nearly seven feet tall, and so skinny. When we were in the village he was using that millet grinder on top of the east hill to pound flour when we saw a cloud of dust rising over the hill on the other side of that valley. The women shouted, "They're coming!" and everyone ran into the high grasses. But Josiah thought, if I can just grind one more bag of meal, if I can just finish this round . . . because he needed the money, you see, to feed his family. He was so greedy. Well, we all ran and hid. Josiah kept grinding. Suddenly those soldiers were coming over the west hill, down into the valley. Josiah dropped that sack so fast when he saw them that a cloud of millet dust flew up from the ground and hung in the air. You should have seen him running for his life, those long limbs flapping wildly as he pelted down the hill towards the grass, leaping over stones and nearly tripping on his own big feet. A strange dance, propelled by fear and gravity.

BOY laughs heartily.

I never saw that man run so fast in all my life. Oh my. That was funny. Flapping all over the place.

BOY imitates Josiah, laughs himself out of breath, then recovers.

Of course they shot him. But, man, he could run.

GIRL stands behind him.

GIRL: Why won't you help? What happened to the man of the house?

BOY: What house?

BOY begins dealing solitaire disinterestedly.

GIRL: Is this what you're going to do? Sit?

BOY: What else is there?

GIRL: We still have to eat, to drink, to wash.

BOY: Why should I sweat? Rations don't need you to plant, to weed, to tend, or harvest. Rations only need you to wait in a line and to extend one hand. A church is not a field. A tent is not a home.

GIRL: Do you think a house will build itself around you if you sit here long enough?

BOY: Do you think you will finally forget if you pretend that you already have?

GIRL: Yes, I have forgotten everything. His mouth, his smell, his strong hands as he touched me, your weak stomach as you watched. I don't remember the four little ones who ran away, the weight of the machete that became like my arm, or the wet sound of them coming apart. I don't remember how you stood aside, how you looked away, and how you covered their faces after. I have forgotten it all.

BOY pushes GIRL to the ground.

BOY: I remember everything. Do you want me to remind you?

MOM: *(off stage)* Girl, will you stoke the fire?

GIRL: It's not her fault she can't remember. She wasn't there.

BOY: Where was she? Where was he? And where is Grandfather now? He is still free, doing as he chooses. And one thousand eyes are on us.

GIRL: Yes, Mom.

GIRL stokes the fire.

BOY: One thousand eyes are on you. Some of them wondering, some of them guessing, and some of them know.

GIRL: Those who know were there beside us.

BOY: I remember how you smiled.

GIRL: How I survived.

BOY: How you laughed.

GIRL: We do what must be done.

BOY: . . . Your field has gone unattended and most of the crop is infected beyond redemption. Will you sit and let it sickly grow, confirming what you know, or burn the field and start again?

GIRL: It won't always be like this. There was a time before this. There has to be a time afterwards too.

BOY: What do you know?

MOM: I have spoken with the teachers. On Monday, you will begin school again. Some people think the best thing is for us to move forward as normally as possible.

SCENE 17: "FACE" TO FACE

BOY adds stones to the pile beside him. GIRL approaches carrying a bucket.

GIRL: Will you come with me to the well?

BOY: Why? No one will take us. We are the takers now.

GIRL: Boy.

BOY: Butcherboy.

GIRL: You changed your name once. Change it again.

BOY: Leave me alone.

GIRL: Do you miss your father?

BOY: Leave me alone.

GIRL: Come to the well with me and I will. I won't talk to you at all. You can walk behind me.

BOY: Just go to the well. Leave me out of it.

GIRL: Uma is here. In this camp. She can't go home either.

BOY: Many people are here.

GIRL: And Uma.

BOY: So?

GIRL: You would let me go alone?

BOY: What business is it of mine? Did you ask me for help when you were kicking those women? Did you need me to walk behind you when you chased those little ones?

GIRL: I did what was necessary—did it for both of us. This is how we survived.

BOY: I did not ask you to do anything for me.

GIRL: I am asking you now to do something for me. Please.

BOY: Come here.

GIRL approaches him.

You want me to do you a favour?

BOY reaches for her.

GIRL jerks away, dropping the bucket.

GIRL: Yes.

BOY: I'll go. If you carry the bucket. Both ways.

GIRL: Alright.

BOY: Go get it.

GIRL: Alright.

GIRL backs towards the bucket.

BOY picks up a stone and whips it at her, intending injury.

Hey.

BOY: Get it.

GIRL tries again, and he whips another stone each time.

Hurry up. It will be dark soon.

GIRL: Come on.

GIRL goes for it again and again until she gets the bucket.

BOY: Alright, go. I'll be behind you, and you can feel what your mercy was like.

GIRL: *(walking)* I miss Dad . . . I miss our house . . . I miss shoes . . . school . . . and laughing . . .

BOY walks a little closer.

I wish he would come for us.

BOY: Quiet.

He stops in sight of the well.

GIRL: Come on.

BOY: I'll wait here. I can see you.

CHORUS sings "Can You Say My Name."

CHORUS: Can you say my name, my name?

UMA enters, cloaked. GIRL and UMA see each other. UMA runs. GIRL chases her. BOY draws water, then goes home. GIRL catches UMA's hand.

GIRL: Uma, I'm pleased to see you here.

UMA tries to tug her hand away.

I mean, I'm not pleased you're here. I'm— I wanted to see you.

UMA tries to tug her hand away.

Please, wait. Please. Talk to me. I won't hurt you. What are you afraid of?

UMA slaps her. She releases UMA's hand.

I'm sorry.

CHORUS: *(sings)* Can I say your name, my name?

UMA gestures.

GIRL: Is your mother here, too?

UMA gestures.

Where . . . ?

UMA gestures.

Burned. I'm sorry. I can't—

UMA: . . .

GIRL unconsciously hurts herself in a small way.

UMA stills her.

GIRL: We never came back here. When the commander needed people to go east I stayed behind with him. We didn't do those things . . . in the village. Always somewhere else. Not innocent people, like at home, but bad people. These people wanted to kill us. We wanted only to live. We never—

UMA touches GIRL's face, then takes GIRL's hand and makes GIRL touch UMA's face.

No more.

She is sick and runs from UMA.

CHORUS hums a verse of "Can You Say My Name."

As close as my hand to your face
Is my life to your word
I live in your mouth
Survive in your remembering
Exist as what I am there
And I can only read the first
I am

BOY: I am
But nothing more
This is a phantom of being

GIRL: I move, unseeing into a thing that is almost familiar

BOY: If running got me nowhere

GIRL: Gone

BOY: Running got me nowhere

GIRL: Uprooted

BOY: Standing still I can't spill blood or tear flesh
I am harmless at rest
This is a test of my will
I am standing / still

GIRL: Still, without breath no motion
Without death / no end

BOY: No end to faces
Looking up, eyes open

GIRL: Better to do it quickly

BOY: Their mouths open

GIRL: Then it is quiet

BOY: Why are we still here?
What more is left for us to do?

SCENE 18: HOW THAT WENT

TEACHER speaks at an outdoor assembly while children stand at attention. UMA holds back, BUSHBABY slung to her body.

TEACHER: Here is a story for you. It is a terrible story. Only two days ago a teacher was walking down this road when three students—two of them are here now—came upon him and beat him and threatened him with a gun. We cannot have teachers with broken bones and bad students hanging around.

Do you know children are very expensive? And some of you children are very bad. It is so hard to earn money. Do you think your parents want to spend their money on bad children who are doing poorly in school?

These days people are kidnapping children, beheading children, defiling children. You have been safe because you are here at school, but when you go into the community, you will be exposed to people. And people do not like children.

You may think that you must be careful of strangers, but in the community even your neighbours may come behind you, throw a sack over your head, and sell you to be sacrificed. Children must stay home!

The passing grade is two hundred. Those of you not achieving that, that is rubbish. You are failing and will continue to fail in life. Look at your report card and you will know who you are.

Quiet down. You, you children there who are talking, that is why you cannot read. There is no such thing as a stupid child, only a child who is not trying. If you had tried you should have been able to succeed.

Now let us recognize those who have been exceptional, those who have worked hard. The rest of you may ask yourselves, what have I done wrong? How has this happened? How can I do better?

You are an embarrassment to this school and an embarrassment to your family. You will see those with green sheets have done very badly indeed. Look around you at your classmates who have failed.

Now you are going to walk back to the classroom. I do not want to see any of you running, and I don't want to see any of you fighting. That is rubbish. We are not going to teach children who will grow up to be murderers and heads of gangs. Instead we will expel you immediately.

You, I know your face. You are a bad one. I expect we will be expelling you soon. Hmph.

Now let us conclude with a joyful song. I hope to hear everybody.

Children sing "The Village Song."

CHILD: Orwan
All we see oh you did make

ALL OTHERS: Orwan
All we give oh you do take

Don't curse the gut for its hunger
Don't curse the field for its grain
Don't curse the sky for its thunder
Don't curse the clouds for its rain

Don't curse the child for its wonder
Don't curse the gourd for its seed
Don't curse the hands for its blunder
Don't curse the sun for its heat

Orwan give
Orwan take
Orwan give
Orwan take
Orwan give
Orwan take

SCENE 19: OF DREAMS

GIRL: Mom asked me what I want to be when I grow up. Can you believe her? I am a mother already.

BOY: Are we going to grow up?

GIRL: I'm afraid so.

BOY: To become what?

GIRL: Whatever we make of ourselves.

MOM wakes and sits outside with GIRL's BABYGIRL. BOY and GIRL sit nearby.

MOM: You are a good baby. You are going to be a lovely girl. Your mother was a very fat baby. She did not eat a lot, but she was always very fat. She was quiet like you, though. Thinking. It is very important for a baby to think about what to do with the rest of her life. There is still so much of it to come. Now, her brother made a lot of noise. His father and I did not sleep for two years after he was born. And her little sister . . .

MOM inhales BABYGIRL's smell.

How does it feel to be so new? I have so much to say to you.

BOY: We have so much to tell each other.

SCENE 20: SEEN ANEW

BOY is sitting by the well, waiting, throwing a rock into the air and catching it. UMA arrives. UMA flinches from BOY, protects BUSHBABY, won't face him. BOY opens his hands to show UMA that they are empty and moves closer. UMA recoils, expecting violence. BOY lowers himself by degrees until UMA is calm enough to indicate she no longer sees BOY as a threat. BOY tells his story from this low position.

BOY: There was a girl, when we were with him. Out there. There was a girl, her eyes were like yours. She was only supposed to carry a message. Only to go with a piece of paper from this person here to that person there. Do you understand? Give me water.

UMA claps: Ayehyeh. Ayehyeh.

She did not run fast enough. The commander struck her, but she was not broken yet, so she yelled. He told me to take her inside. To take her. Inside. And she cried. I told her to stop it, but she kept looking at me. She would not close her eyes and only kept looking at me. Give me water.

UMA claps: Ayehyeh. Ayehyeh.

The commander was in the doorway, watching us. He said to me, "She will continue to look at you as long as she can see." He asked me, "What are you going to do?" I told the girl again. "Close your eyes." But she wouldn't. Give me water.

UMA claps: Ayehyeh. Ayehyeh.

I finished with her and she still kept looking. The commander gave me a short stick, and then she could no longer see, and I could no longer see what she thought of me. I am part of what happened to you, and you are part of what happened to me. That will always be true. I want you to look at me.

UMA turns. BOY drops the stone. They embrace for a long time.

SCENE 21: SOMEBODY GETS ERT

ANCESTOR: But the waterfall said:
"This sin is not mine,"
and the buffalo were blameless,
the mountain itself denied.
Released of the spirit within my flesh
I stand outside this unrest.
And seek to know the hands that struck this blow.
Not mine, the strike that split the earth.
Not mine to grant rebirth.

This first stone is not the road,
this first coin is not what is owed.
No more can this weight be shed
than it be shared.

BOY and GIRL speak to fellow students/ex-soldiers in the schoolyard.

BOY: I have spoken to Uma . . . I have looked into her eyes and seen myself. I am not an animal, nor am I a helpless child. I am a man, and what I have done is not all that I am. What you have done is not all that you are. We are nothing until we know that. We can't stay confined here anymore. If we must be alive then let us live.

I know what you have done, as you know what I have done. I know you as your mother, your father, your God does not know you:

without judgment. You can tell me everything and I will ask you nothing.

What can we do with all those things they cannot understand? With the things they could not stand to hear if we told them? With the things they want us to forget, that we cannot help remembering? Let us tell them to each other. Let us forgive and find mercy. For all of those who cannot know you, I know you.

This is my sister. You know what she has done, and what has been done to her. You call her defiled. My sister is not defiled—she is sacred. She is alive. She has created life; this makes her ultimately powerful. From today my sister will be called Hajjera because she is powerful.

ALL sing "Can You Say My Name."

ALL: Can you say my name, my name . . . my name
Can I say my name, my name . . . my name

As close as my hand is to your face
Is my life to your word
I live in your mouth
Survive in your remembering

The waterfall said:
"This sin is not mine"
The buffalo were blameless
The mountain itself denied
I wanna know
The hands that struck this blow
Not mine: the strike that split the earth
Not mine: the one to grant rebirth

Can you say my name, my name . . . my name.
Can I say my name, my name . . . my name.

GIRL: My mother taught me Te'mento. She taught me this:

The beauty is in the rising
but to rise you must come low.
You can go so low that you
are beneath the earth.
But you must always rise above the place
where you began.
You rise
because you cannot stay down.

They dance with strength.

SCENE 22: HOMEGOING

MOM: Perhaps your father has returned. We should go home.

BOY: The crops will be dry and withered.

GIRL: Everything is burned. Our house no longer stands.

MOM: Then it is time to rebuild.

GIRL: Let us build something new.

They walk towards home. BOY *turns back, looks to the sky, reaches in his pocket and throws a stone. They walk off, the community gathers in.*

EPILOGUE: A HARD RAIN

A stone echoes down the drainpipe as the scene dims and ANCESTOR *is seen rolling a stone in hand and pocketing it.*

ANCESTOR: I threw the stone that came before
Its weight in my hand was a pebble, no more
No one knows what wind it was that made it soar
Or what weight it has left to pour.

Fin.

Bring my Babies Home

Lyrics: DM St. Bernard
Music: DM St. Bernard & Pamela Gilmartin
Transcription: Jenna Geen

Can You Say My Name

Lyrics: DM St. Bernard & Maddie Bautista
Music: Maddie Bautista
Transcription: Jenna Geen

Feet Don't Fail Me Now

Lyrics: DM St. Bernard
Music: DM St. Bernard & Pamela Gilmartin
Transcription: Jenna Geen

♩ = 90

11
CHOR.
rest for the wick-ed, no, no Don't. Don't
CHILD.
rest for the wick-ed, no, no Four years and one life - time
13
CHOR.
Feet don't fail me now. Don't. Don't.
CHILD.
Feet don't fail me now On - ly think a-bout one life: mine
15
CHOR.
Feet don't fail me now Don't. Don't.
CHILD.
Feet don't fail me now Can't see an end - ing, give me a sign
17
CHOR.
Feet don't fail me now No rest for the wick-ed, no, no No
CHILD.
Feet don't fail me now No rest for the wick-ed, no, no No
19
CHOR.
rest for the wick-ed, no, no Don't. Don't
CHILD.
rest for the wick-ed, no, no Don't. Don't.

21
CHOR.
Feet don't fail me now. Don't. Don't.
CHILD.
Feet don't fail me now. Don't. Don't.
23
CHOR.
Feet don't fail me now. Don't. Don't.
CHILD.
Feet don't fail me now. Don't. Don't.
25
CHOR.
Feet don't fail me now No rest for the wick ed, no, no No
CHILD.
Feet don't fail me now No rest for the wick-ed, no, no No
27
CHOR.
rest for the wick-ed, no, no
CHILD.
rest for the wick-ed, no, no Four years and one life - time
(whispered)

Prayer of the Gun

Lyrics: DM St.Bernard & Maddie Bautista
Music: Maddie Bautista
Transcription: Jenna Geen

L.
CHOR.
bone Caught in the throat Of a mem ory A
days, for nights No eat, no bite No rest, just fight For
hole At the bot tom of the boat
days, for nights No eat, no bite No rest, just fight For
Leav-ing re al men to drown and fab - les to float
days, for nights No eat, no bite Cut my feet, crush my head,
fab - les to float
Sweat my tears, bleed my bread, Cut my feet, crush my head, Sweat my tears, bleed my bread,
LEAD + CHORUS:
Cut my feet, crush my head, sweat my tears, bleed my bread Stone in to
blade, bran ches to shaft Make me for one thing

36
CHOR.
on ly oh Ar wa (oh___ Ar - wa)
39
CHOR.
Stone in to blade, bran ches to
42
CHOR.
spoken: ayeyeh!
shaft Make me for one thing on ly

Run to the Fields

Lyrics: DM St. Bernard
Music: DM St. Bernard & Pamela Gilmartin
Transcription: Jenna Geen

Running for Life

Lyrics: DM St. Bernard
Music: DM St. Bernard & Pamela Gilmartin
Transcription: Jenna Geen

The Stone's Ripple

Lyrics: DM St. Bernard and Maddie Bautista
Music: Maddie Bautista
Transcription: Jenna Geen

♩ = 100

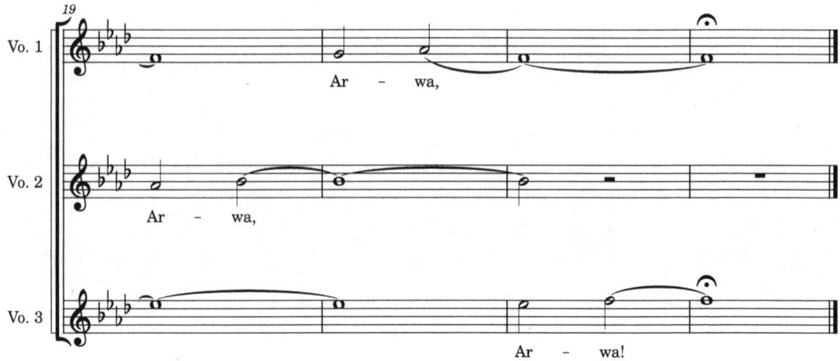
19
Vo. 1
Ar - wa,
Vo. 2
Ar - wa,
Vo. 3
Ar - wa!

The Village Song

Lyrics: DM St. Bernard & Maddie Bautista
Music: Maddie Bautista
Transcription: Jenna Geen

31
LEAD
Don't curse the child for its won-der
CHORUS
Don't curse the cloud for its rain
35
LEAD
Don't curse the gourd for its seed
Don't curse the hands for its blun-der
39
LEAD
Don't curse the sun for its heat
CHORUS
Don't curse the child for its won-der
43
CHORUS
Don't curse the gourd for its seed
Don't curse the hands for its blun-der
47
repeat x3
LEAD
Or - wan give
CHORUS
Or - wan take
Don't curse the sun for its heat

ACKNOWLEDGEMENTS

(DEVELOPMENT CONTRIBUTORS)

Storygivers: Mercie Banche Onyut, Jimmy Okello, Patrick Akera, Geoffrey Omony, Hajjera, Saad, and countless unnameable others.

Dramaturgy: Isaac Thomas, Sarah Garton Stanley, Keira Loughran, Yvette Nolan.

Workshop Actors (various occasions): Awaovieyi Agie, Peter N. Bailey, Lisa Karen Cox, Rita Shelton Deverell, Miranda Edwards, Lili Francks, Julien Hyacinthe, Marcia Johnson, Joan Kivanda, Araya Mengesha, Idil Mussa, Clare Preuss, Camille Lesley-Ann Walker, Kashka Wyatt, the National Arts Centre English Theatre Ensemble (Petrina Bromley, Christine Brubaker, Dmitry Chepovetsky, David Coomber, Eric Davis, Leah Doz, Sheldon Elter, Quancetia Hamilton, Eliza-Jane Scott, Joey Tremblay), Dante Jemmott, Mark Cassius, Kwaku Okyere.

Design and Composition: Christian Hurst, Pamela Gilmartin, Rachel Forbes, Maddie Bautista, Tawiah Ben M'Carthy, Yvette Nolan, Michelle Ramsay, Cameron Davis, Jeff Chief.

High-Pressure Encouragement From: Brenda St. Bernard, Kern Albert, Gein Wong, Sarah Garton Stanley, Jillian Keiley, Yvette Nolan.

Donna-Michelle St. Bernard, a.k.a. Belladonna the Blest, is an emcee, playwright, agitator, and practitioner of humanitarian arts. Her main body of work, the 54ology, includes *Cake*, *Sound of the Beast*, *A Man A Fish*, *Salome's Clothes*, *Gas Girls*, *Give It Up*, *The Smell of Horses*, *Bilguisa Speaks Up*, *Diggers*, *Conjugal*, *Hunt/Peck*, and *The First Stone*. She is a contributor to *The Only Good Indian* (Jiv Parasram, Tom Arthur Davis/Pandemic Theatre), *Forbidden* (Afarin Mansouri/Tapestry Opera), and *Oubliette* (Ivan Barbotin/Tapestry Opera). Other theatre works include *Reaching For Starlight*, *They Say He Fell*, and *The Final Inquiry*. She is co-editor with Yvette Nolan of *Refractions: Solo* (2014) and *Refractions: Scenes* (2020) and editor of *Indian Act: Residential School Plays* (2018), all published with Playwrights Canada Press.

Maddie Bautista (she/her) is a Bi, Saudi Arabia–born Filipina sound designer and composer based in Treaty 13, Tkaronto. In the daytime, you can catch Maddie creating and shaping sound in iconic theatres across the country—from composing original music in the earliest stages of new work development, to tuning systems with live musicians and mid-sized casts. She has created music and sound design for over eighty productions and counting across Canada, for theatres such as the Stratford Festival, Alberta Theatre Projects, the Grand Theatre, Theatre Aquarius, Soulpepper, Tarragon Theatre, and more. After the sun goes down, she moonlights as half of xLq with Jordan Campbell—a queer pop performance duo who tours across the country with their daring, interactive theatre and bizarre, grungy drag. Maddie received two Dora Mavor Moore Awards for *Love You Wrong Time* (Outstanding Sound Design and Composition and Outstanding Ensemble). www.maddiebautista.com.